~~~~~~~~~~

FEELING HUMAN

~~~~~~~~~~

by Susi Bocks

Artwork by
Terry Susi

Feeling Human
Copyright © 2017 by Susi Bocks
All Rights Reserved

Cover Art by Susi Bocks
Artwork by Terry Susi

www.IWriteHer.com

Printed in the United States

ISBN-13:
978-1522822172

ISBN-10:
1522822178

To Mendy, my sister. Our relationship has delved into all these emotions except one.

Acknowledgements

The person I would like to acknowledge and thank most profusely is the artist - Terry Susi. Her contribution made this a collaboration of love. She's my BFF, so talented, supportive and such an inspiration to me! Working together with her on this project was indeed one of the best moments in my life. Thank you, thank you and thank you so much for going down this path with me.

The next person in line deserving of deep affection from me is my husband, Uwe. Without his support (literally and figuratively), and his valuable input this would never have become a reality. Thank you for giving me space, time and your encouragement to do what makes me happy.

My children, Sean and Julian, although not necessarily avid readers of the things I produce, I think they have always been secretly proud of their mother. I thank them so much for believing in me. Much of my personal growth is because of them as our shared experiences have given me so much material to work with over the years! Thank you, boys, for giving me substance in my life.

David Fitzgerald, you have been an inspiration to me since we first met many years ago. Not only have you always been supportive of my efforts, whatever they may be, but you've been that push I needed to help me move forward in making this happen. I thank you for your advice, your guidance and our friendship. To Kristen Reynolds who took time out of her busy life to help me shape what this book ultimately became. I appreciate you and thank you for being selfless. Shannon Kietzman, you made me a better writer because of your efforts. I can't thank you enough.

I'd be remiss in not also acknowledging the people who were consistently supportive of my writing, whether my blogs or when I published pieces for other organizations. Thank you for being my cheering section all along. You are all one of the reasons this book saw the light of day.

An acknowledgment goes to all the people who have contributed somehow to me experiencing these emotions. Whether detrimental or positive, they influenced who I became. For that, I am eternally grateful. You have no idea how much valuable insight you bestowed on me. I gained what I needed to learn, and realized so much more about you.

Hats off to another writer - Vera Nazarian - for allowing me to include a piece of her work in this compilation. Her poetry added much to what I was trying to say.

A very special shout-out to Google! Without you, my research would have been incredibly tedious and mind-numbing.

And lastly, Josiah Mannion, my thanks for the last piece in getting this book to its final stages before publication. I appreciate your eye for making beautiful pictures and your warm and caring friendship.

Preface

People, their emotions and what they put out to the world - their story - has always been a fascinating subject to me. I wanted to capture what it meant to feel human in an all-encompassing way. The idea for this short compilation of essays, poetry, and art came about while pondering how to explain human emotions. Not just mine, but the universal condition of feelings. My wish was to highlight those experiences by all who inhabit this world.

While I only have my perspective on what it feels like to be me, I also wanted to understand the emotions of the average person. My goal was to then bring together my thoughts with theirs about the primary feelings we all experience. In addition to expressing these emotions in words, I have included beautiful artwork to offer a visual perspective of each feeling at the beginning of each chapter. I intended to give the reader a deeper immersion into these emotions so they can experience them fully. I can only hope I succeeded in accomplishing this goal.

The Process of Identifying Emotions
To determine which emotions were the most relevant to people, I created a survey referencing forty-two different human emotions. While the anonymous survey was admittedly rather unscientific and informal, participants completed an online survey in which they selected the top

five emotions they experience the most often. A total of one hundred and seventy-six people responded, the majority of which I do not know personally. Based on the survey results, I identified the top ten human emotions: frustration, love, empathy, anxiety, compassion, interest, acceptance, affection, anger and depression. The percentage of participants who identified experiencing each of these emotions was as follows:

- Frustration: 41.5%
- Love: 41.5%
- Empathy: 35.2%
- Anxiety: 30.7%
- Compassion: 30.7%
- Interest: 27.8%
- Acceptance: 21.6%
- Affection: 21.6%
- Anger: 19.3%
- Depression: 19.3%

To see the statistics play out this way was interesting to me as I've always felt life is a constant struggle to find the balance between opposing forces.

The Layout

The chapters in this book take the reader on a literary journey where each emotion is analyzed, including discussing the benefit or detriment of each emotion. Each essay followed with poetry showing us how they feel. While many of the thoughts in this writing derive from my own experiences, the inspiration also comes from the emotional interactions I have experienced and witnessed in others throughout my lifetime. I asked a dear-to-my-heart artist friend who produces beautiful work to help me visually conceptualize how these emotions feel on a canvas. Each chapter is set in motion with her work. I think she did a fantastic job!

As you go through the chapters, I encourage you to explore your responses to the emotions and imagery the book creates for you. I hope this is a positive experience as you revel in those emotions that contribute to your own life. May those that profoundly affect you help you to make some meaningful changes in your life. Above all, I hope you enjoy the creative efforts as much as we did while thinking about and pulling together this collaborative project of love. The bonus was seeing it become a reality.

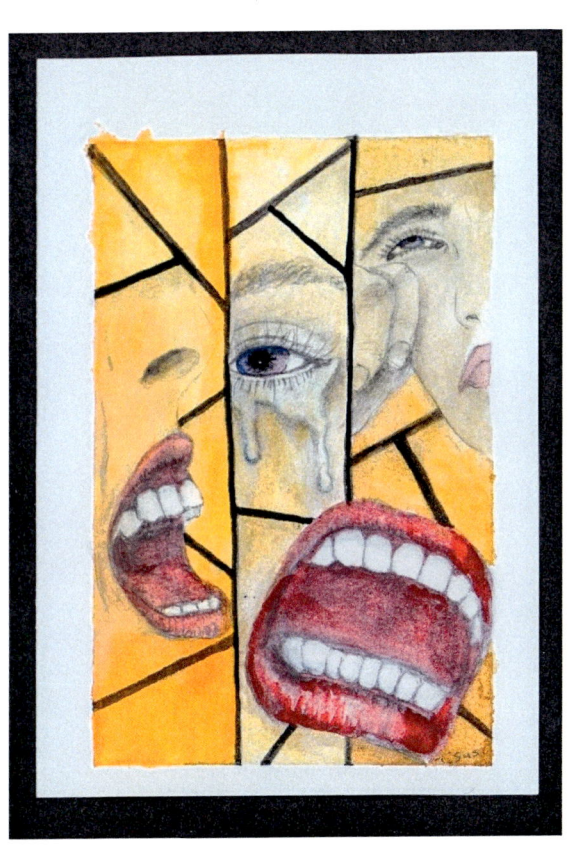

Frustration

The initial response of this emotion means having a healthy respect for ourselves. We feel threatened, and then we react. It is the response when something or someone has affected us, after being subjected to an event of which we want no part. It isn't in our plans. We expect it to alter so that we may continue along the path we're heading, whatever that may have been. It's a derailment that won't likely self-correct. It requires us to intercede and find a resolution. We don't like to do that, and we don't think we should have to put in the effort when we didn't create the situation in the first place. Managing this is partly where the frustration arises. In most cases, we are just frustrated when we encounter situations we don't think we should have to endure.

We can also feel frustrated when we are unable to resolve a situation. We feel we are stuck in the wrong place, at the wrong time, for too long. Other people may add to the frustration with their problems or when they aren't listening, hearing or comprehending what we need them to understand. Frustration is also an expression of mini-anger at ourselves or the world around us for standing in our way. This self-hate can push us to the verge of giving up. Defeat sets in giving way to a gloomier emotion, such as depression.

We know it is annoying to deal with an individual or situation that creates a roadblock responsible for propelling an event in a direction that was not on our radar. Not meeting expectations mean frustration occurs. The inability to change or achieve something can impact us deeply, but it also all depends on what intrudes in our lives to create this reaction. That situation will determine our level of response. The run-in with a cashier who is being petty can be frustrating to be sure, but having a wife or a husband who continually spends all the hard-earned money brought into the relationship would likely elicit a much deeper frustration, possibly bordering on rage. Each scenario where we feel frustration and exactly what it means to us personally will determine how much we fight for it or how long it will take before we can move on.

Frustrations can also stem from the prevention of the progression of ideas, things that are thwarting the success we are trying to achieve. It's the constant challenge of overcoming small or big problems besieging the best-laid plans. Having a mindset that informs us this is normal in facing challenges, understanding there will be setbacks in the course of achieving progress, can help prevent frustration from breeding defeat.

The unhealthiness of frustration is feeling this emotion because of a crisis or situation that occurs in what could have otherwise been a good day. It requires action and resolution to overcome. Internalizing frustration breeds fear, anxiety and depression. Continually feeling frustrated and repressing it is just as frustrating as making an effort and waiting for a resolution that never comes. Both situations result in consistently wasting our precious time and energy, leaving us feeling dissatisfied. In the long-term, it is draining to our physical and emotional well-being when our efforts to change the situation prove to be worthless.

All types of circumstances can be the catalyst for those feelings of dissatisfaction, exasperation and even downright anger when hopes get thwarted, wishes are dashed, and we experienced the prevention of progress. There can be a deep disappointment felt in that frustration as well. Menial, mundane tasks that don't go as expected can be just as infuriating, not just those moments where our needs are not met.

Whatever those conditions bring to the forefront of our day, the best way to avoid getting sucked deeper into frustration is to breathe and work to understand what is going on. Give the person who is standing in our way the benefit of the doubt. If he or she did something unintentionally, they more than likely feel miserable about having been a catalyst for the current crappiness you are both experiencing. The person doesn't need more heaped upon him. Frankly, frustration won't solve the problem. Rather, it could lead to better communication with the other person and a quicker resolution of the situation.

For those situations over which we have no control, do realize that just responding with frustration isn't going to be a healthy response. Chronic unfulfilled needs and continued dissatisfaction will lead to darker emotions or insecurities and could be the start of a fall into a downward spiral. This descent can be more unmanageable to deal with than just frustration. Trying to identify allies in those situations and get the support we need can be daunting, but they may be able to help us guide us in choosing to pursue a new and different path, the direction of which one we can control.

Prelude to Tears

I greet you with a smile, and love in my heart.
Our holding pattern lasts longer than I thought it would.
There's joy in my eyes again. I think I see it in yours?
Our time now recaptures old memories.
For a moment.
Distant hurts begin to emerge; impatient attitudes reveal themselves.
That's what was in your eyes.
It's not a reconnection; it's the battlefield. All over again.
The unresolvable will continue.
My face grits tight, my body tenses, gearing up the protective shields.
The venom within flaring up, spilling over into the once calm mood.
Agitation prevails, and displeasure dominates once again.
The look in our eyes, once filled with love, glazed over again with annoyance.
We yell. We fight. We retreat.
You leave, and I cry.

Same Shit, Different Day

Cue the frustrated tone... and go...

Feed me, change me; I don't know what I need.

Wah Wah Wah

I can't do it

Wait for me, hold me, pick me up

I want candy

Let me do it

No, I won't share my toys

Hey, why does he have a bigger scoop than me

Why doesn't anybody like me

Girls suck

Boys suck

Notice me

Teachers suck

Stop teasing me

Why am I crying

Cramps suck

Why won't he call

How could you do this to me

She doesn't like me

Leave me alone

Are you listening to me

You just don't understand me

Parents suck

I hate you

I'm done with you, I'm outta here
Why does everything cost so much
I need a better job
Damn car
Bosses suck
It's raining on our wedding day
You spend too much money, you save too much
I'm nauseous, ugh - acid indigestion, I want to cry, my feet are so swollen
Stop crying, stop pooping, stop puking
Quiet, I'm on the phone
Get down from there
Stop whining
You did what
I thought I knew you
I'm done, alone again
I need a new refrigerator
Dating sucks
Taxes are just too damn high
The house needs a new roof
Everything just costs so much
I need a better job
Where has all the time gone, there's still so much I want to do
I want to retire now
Work sucks
My back hurts, my bones ache
I'm sick, I'm dying...

Life is one long list of frustrations; from the time we are born until we die. We'll struggle with roadblocks put in our way, many people - either loved ones or strangers, consequences of others actions, day to day situations, ineptitude, nature, inanimate objects, our failures and consequences.

It's like our existence is a good meal and the waiter wants to fresh ground pepper it way too much.

Post Un-intention

Your actions were unintentional.
They hurt anyway.

You said you would never do this intentionally,
That would make you a monster.

Your integrity was lacking, just like your apology.
My will is lacking now, and my disappointment is immense.

Your unintentionally created abyss is gaping.
I don't know if we'll survive the fall.

You're looking up for redemption,
I'm looking down deeper into the hole where you left me.

You say you'll do anything,
Then do the right things. Intentionally.

Grrrrrr...

Love

It is a term that we have struggled to define for centuries, and yet, it fills volumes of poetry, film, and song. It's a word expressed so often, many times not even appropriately. Nonetheless, it does signal a connection that needs exposure in the public spectrum. In intensely private and extremely close relationships, it becomes a very personal definition that tends to play out predictably with the two people involved.

Love is a warm connection. It brings comfort to us and provides a feeling of safety while also creating a tenderness and obligation to that person. A smile creeps into your heart, and your stomach flops when you see the one you love. It's the ability to understand yourself through their eyes. You feel uplifted with their support and efforts. Being loved means you are wanted and needed. Loving knows it is a commitment to get to the other side of shitty. They are on your side, always were and always will be.

How we love informs the world who we are. One can sense the generosity in those who are loving to others, their kindness and contributions to others less fortunate are evident by the appreciation they leave in their wake. Random gestures for good and intentional giving are all signs of one who loves, respects and appreciates humanity and the world where we reside. It is greatness within an individual who would give what is so desperately needed.

It can be momentary and brief, inspiring us to greater choices and giving us a nudge in a better direction. Possibly, it can also make us long to be committed and enjoy a long-lasting relationship. In each case, there is an enthusiasm brought out in us for the connection made. It can be one-sided, in some cases intentional or just because there is no way to come together to form a relationship. Still, the attraction is there and admiration can grow along with that attraction or interest for the person of our affection.

In situations of reciprocated love, the relationship projects outward a closeness and intimacy that seems to be shared by only them. It is a close connection seemingly comprised of so many other emotions rolled together tightly to describe all that they feel for that person: joy, compassion, interest, excitement, tenderness, passion, warmth and so much more. It's an emotion experienced by friends, significant others, partners, mothers and fathers, children - any person with which you allow yourself to feel an intense and intimate bond. A connection that is hard to walk away from or sever.

They say love is what makes the world go round. I would posit love is what makes us go round.

You are Always Here with Me

There's ease in our relationship, a luxurious comfort even when our lives don't intersect. I've forgotten some of the histories we've shared, but your impression on me has never diminished.

The essence of our relationship is and always has been encouragement, whether near or far, involved or silent. We forged a bond a lifetime ago by being each other's hero. Through our friendship, our experience of finding stability within each other gave us some peace from the turmoil we lived. The acceptance we found with each other for our personhood was something we both desperately needed; it was the first bit of strength we gave to each other. We added to that foundation separately throughout our lifetime experiences to become the women we are today. Wholeness, finally. Proud of who we are, living and enjoying the good things life has to offer, loving the people who deserve our love and thoroughly enjoying who we have become.

I'd not realized until recently how much of an impact our childhood friendship had on me and how much we mentored each other through those times. It was valuable to me.

We've discarded the broken shells we were a lifetime ago and have gone through some incredible situations since then, but we have not stopped showing life we're not going down without a fight.

I so do appreciate you sharing that part of you that I carry around with me always.

I thought you should know that.

Feeling Incomplete and Suffering

We will all struggle to love; the right emotions aren't present, and the wrong ones preside.

Experience resulting in pain leaves us with a constant struggle to not hate the new. If there is desire, but it projects fear, there is no acceptance.

Without empathy for others, it places selfish expectations at the forefront. If not met, there is no understanding.

Giving others the room to blossom in their greatness is necessary. Without doing so, there is no appreciation.

Healing past hurts is essential. Gathering the courage to trust again closes old wounds. Standing proudly to be yourself while lifting up others will complete the triangle. Only when you accept yourself, understand who you are and appreciate what you contribute uniquely to this world will you be able to give what is needed in return. It is then when you will no longer suffer, feel incomplete or struggle with love.

"Love is made up of three unconditional properties in equal measure:

1. Acceptance
2. Understanding
3. Appreciation

Remove any one of the three, and the triangle falls apart. Which, by the way, is something highly inadvisable. Think about it — do you really want to live in a world of only two dimensions? So, for the love of a triangle, please keep love whole."

Vera Nazarian
The Perpetual Calendar of Inspiration

Happy Anniversary, Lover

19 years ago, we didn't celebrate our wedding day except to kiss briefly, murmur "I love you" and pay the clerk to have the Justice of the Peace perform the ceremony. We were on our lunch hour, and I was eight months pregnant suffering from a severe case of acid indigestion. I wasn't entirely happy that day, and I'd say we were both more relieved than anything else because your first marriage was finally legally dissolved and we were able to tie the knot officially. We could go on with our lives and get married, which would allow me to get your insurance to cover the impending delivery of our child. Before you begin to think that I'm not grateful that I am where I am today with you, understand I would have done anything to be together with you. I didn't need a marriage ceremony to make me stay. Getting married was just one aspect of what we did together to form this union that we symbolically celebrate every year. After being together for over two decades now, the wedding ceremony was just the least memorable of it all.

These past years string together warm, kind, uplifting, passionate, loving, intimate, open, dark, scary, life-changing, devastating, solidifying, agonizing, fearful, strength-filled, supportive, mature, soulful, and thousands of more interwoven terms to describe our still on-going relationship. Or, as I would call it, our mutually agreed upon decision to create a union that would challenge all others I've ever known. We decided to be Team Bocks – you, me and our kids.

Just like all couples, we've had our ups and downs over the years. Some moments have been excruciatingly hard to bear – being on either side of the extreme of living will feel that way. Exhilarating happiness can ache just as much as a devastating betrayal. We've experienced both. We've survived both. We have managed to maneuver our way into a calm, reassuring, and content state of mind with each other. I would like to say that I have enjoyed living through all these times with you, but I can't. Some moments sucked, and I didn't think we'd make it. To end up here 20 years later and with our union intact. Well, that means a lot to me.

Thank you for being patient with me and for staying by my side through the good and the bad. You didn't just give lip service. You have truly been there with me, with your whole body and mind. You were there when hugs were needed. You provided shoulders and arms for tear-filled moments. You reached out your hands to give support during uncertain times. You have been there for me emotionally through my most painful moments, even while in your despair. You sometimes took a backseat when you felt my needs were greater. You have also been there to celebrate my successes and share in my good fortunes. You are the one person who I want to share these moments with because they are divinely sweeter when you are there.

Of course, our decision for coupledom has not only affected you and me but also impacted our progeny. I thank you for not only providing a haven for me but our children as well. We weren't perfect parents, but together we gave our kids what you and I never had: a stable relationship they could count on and a loving home. Thank you for giving them the foundation they needed for a chance at a better future. That means a lot to me.

The thing that now means the most to me is that who I am to you today is still the same as 20 years ago. You still have the same love, admiration, and respect for me as an individual now as you did then, even though we've come through things in our union that has changed us, for better or worse. You still accept me and love me for who I am. You've made it clear to me that I'm your priority. I get it, and I thank you deeply for your unwavering support of me, the person. You've managed to show me what so many others couldn't and didn't. I am loved, I have value, and I'm worthy of so much more than what I received at times.

I don't know what our future holds. There is no crystal ball for anyone. I'm just thankful knowing I had this relationship and got to be wrapped up in it.

Thank you, my love.

Empathy

With all of the tragedies, mishaps, and ill-timed natural events taking place every day, it is fortunate that we can experience empathy. Many probably wouldn't be able to handle all the crisis' which are sent their way without the intervention and caring of others. Having friends, and even strangers, choose to identify with these situations and calm those who are suffering around them helps those who are suffering get over their drama more effectively than they would if no attention were given to them at all.

Having someone who can understand your feelings or your situation is something that some term as being a "blessing." In some moments, it genuinely feels that way. Often, people can't imagine that anyone would be concerned enough about their welfare to feel their pain with them. Their lack of self-worth contributes to this feeling. It is uplifting when you know someone is on your side and understands your desperation. It is a relief to know that someone cares enough to help you get through a desperate time. Evidence of this is in the form of an encouraging smile, a tight squeeze on the shoulder or a full-on body hug. Tears can flow easily knowing the person is there to support you, allowing you to work through what you are feeling. It is a trust-filled bond at that moment. It brings with it both relief and safety.

For the person who is experiencing empathy, there is a feeling of oneness with the individual who is suffering. Feeling empathy allows you to identify with them in their dire situation that is causing them pain, either emotional, mental or physical. This sense of identity, triggered by a shared experience or a deep-rooted sense of caring for others and where they are at that moment, brings forth an emotional response. The empathetic response can range from merely acknowledging that you understand what the person is going through to becoming emotionally involved with and intentionally nurturing the other person. The pain of others can resonate deep within the individual, evoking the response of deep caring. It can also lead to an offer of help or simply a listening ear, which can give the sufferer hope that their situation will pass. A person can experience empathy without being compassionate, but cannot be compassionate without empathy.

Sadly, there are those who take advantage of empathetic people who suffer right along with the distraught. In these situations, the callous ones dust themselves off as soon as the crisis has passed and the caring individual is left behind to cope with the shallowness of the drama-filled person. When desperation strikes once more, that person may return to tap into the empathy of their friend. It is the depressing cycle of use and abuse of those who feel deeply for the welfare of others. It's a selfish act, not an opportunity for two people to connect, or for the empathetic person to shine. Rather, it is a situation where the only intention is for the sufferer to enjoy personal gain. We should be wary of those who create their chaos, who use our resources and make us feel guilty because we haven't "done enough" for them. These individuals always seem to need and want help, but we should be careful not to let them suck us dry and leave our spirits empty. What's needed more in those situations is a lowered impulse to respond. A strong dose of honesty about their actions could prove detrimental to your connection, but it just might help them see the error of their ways. More importantly, vulnerable empaths are saved from the emotional destruction caused by those types.

People who have empathy for others will react to the suffering they see in others. It hurts them to see individuals or animals in horrific situations of devastation, sadness, injustice or desperation. They don't want anyone or anything to be in pain. When they do witness pain, empathetic people are there for those who are suffering, even if what they are going through is the only form of acknowledgment. Even though they are not directly affected by the situation, empaths are affected by the suffering they see. They experience the pain right along with those who were initially disturbed, and they feel pain in response to those who are in need. Their anguish shows care and concern for others, with the goal being to alleviate the struggles for both the sufferer and the empath.

What a sad world we would live in if we didn't have empathetic people. They are the types we need a whole lot more of sometimes.

I Don't Like You, But I Care

Why are you hateful?
I see your fear, let me help.
I understand you.

Your Hurt Is My Hurt

There I go, minding my own business.
Life is good, a smile on my face.
Things to do. Doing them.

It all comes to a screeching halt.
My outlook just got less rosy.
My insides face a shock.

It's you I see. It's you I feel.
The picture of you is somehow off.
I can tell.

Your body, your eyes, your hands making motions that aren't normally you.

My hand on yours, my arm around your shoulders.
Let me understand. Let me in.
Let me help.

You got bad news.
Devastating, unexpected, and life-altering.
It cuts you deep, and I have an open wound now.

You're crying; I'm crying with you.
Your sobbing grows, so does mine.

I want to hold you til it all goes away.

Your pain is my pain.

I will cradle it in my bosom until it dissipates from yours.

Until I see your smile, only then will I release it.

And you will feel better.

So will I.

Soon, I hope.

You Found Me in My Pain

The despair, the hopelessness. It fills the room around me. I echo a chamber of sorrow. Rocking keeps me in motion, not settling in on any one thing bringing me down. It keeps me from giving up and giving in to complete uncertainty.

How can it change? When will it end? What will I do? I don't know. I'm so lost right now. My compass is broken. I feel so exposed, so raw. I'm shielded from nothing. It all takes its toll, chipping away at me more and more. I will be broken soon.

But then you're here with me, in my space. You reach out, purposefully. I feel a smidgen of relief. Some of my burden is lifted, creating a pocket of ease and a small wave of calm. Your gentleness with my broken psyche lets me breathe. You understand my agony. You cover my uncertainty. You protect me. I see in your eyes a sense of knowing and concern. There's a deep and genuine focus within you; it knows I need you. My intensity of dysfunction matches your strong emotional support. You create an atmosphere that blankets my frailty with kindness. I respond with relief.

My remarkable friend, my ally, and comfort. I cherish your protection from what is causing me pain. My deep appreciation comes from seeing your love match and overpower my distress. Your guidance takes me out of my desperate and frenzied life; it brings me back to a place of determined direction. All the while I'm feeling your strength and your care supporting me. You know where I am inside, buried beneath the layers of pain. Your tears understand I need an ally.

You saw me in my state and reached out where I was. Never mind what was going on in your life. You surrounded me with warmth and caring. You understood the weight of the space I occupied, and what I needed.

Thank you. I can rise above it now.

Anxiety

Anxiety can be as slight as the feeling you get when facing an annoying agitation with an unknown outcome, or it can be as significant as a full-blown panic attack. You may feel mildly out of tune, or you may feel incapacitated. Much of how we react to these worrisome situations of uncertainty depends on our unique chemical makeup as well as our learned coping skills. Traditionally, we think of anxiety as being such an extreme reaction that we are left feeling debilitated and unable to control anything. In reality, being worried or fretful over something is nature's way of telling us we are concerned about what will happen. Having an episode of anxiety can help to get us moving in the direction necessary to ensure things work out. This caring in thought motivates us to action, which can ultimately be a positive experience. Though it may not feel like it at the time, this form of anxiety can be beneficial.

This emotion can create a temporary upheaval in the lives of those who suffer from occasional bouts. During this time, the person might feel like things are out of their control. They may feel devastated by a crisis. Or, they may be anticipating the worst due to events taking place in their lives. Anxiety plays into those situations rather effortlessly, as one can feel overwhelmed and unable to take charge of the situation. On the other hand, they might be able to easily resolve the problem and find relief from the anxiety once the anxiety-producing event is no longer an issue.

Angst presents itself emotionally, but can also manifest itself physically. It can leave you feeling tense, nervous or shaky, or it can feel like a surge of electric energy, heightening and intensifying your concern or worry about something. Imagine a strong, forceful wind ripping through the branches of a tree; the leaves tossed about indiscriminately, the sounds of the rustling bordering on screaming; the surge of wind in nature is what an intense anxiety attack can resemble. It is a force to be reckoned with. There is a fearfulness, the 'fight or flight' response can be triggered as well. You might experience agitation, or you might feel perturbed, creating a feeling of apprehension and extreme unease. Many times there can be a desire for some action to take place, but then you feel stymied by an overwhelming sense of doom. Quite possibly leaving you to stare quietly and fixating on something in your view, not one sound escaping you. It's just you in your head. It can overcome you to the point of lethargy and depression.

Out of control anxiety may present as an extreme feeling of physical danger or terror. The experience of feeling a possible heart attack or other dramatic symptoms such as dizziness, rapid heartbeat, chest pains or a feeling of being totally out of control. This experience mimics symptoms of real consequences of a health issue but is, in reality, a panic attack. It can feel so serious that you may believe you are on the brink of death. As a result of these feelings, many people who struggle with anxiety also experience frequent emergency room visits. A panic attack is an extreme reaction to the manifestation of uncontrolled anxiety. During a panic attack, it can be difficult to distinguish whether the physical reaction is something genuinely consequential and life-altering or just an out of control anxiety response to stressors.

Experiencing imagined medical crises' is not the only extreme form of anxiety you may endure. A change in the perception of reality during those situations can also occur, creating a very distorted view of what is happening around you. To add to the problem, you experience additional anxiety as you worry about how those around you are perceiving your response. You find yourself hoping your body will somehow mask the internal turmoil that is intensifying beneath your skin as you try to contain the reactions you are experiencing. This scenario creates, even more, anxiety, a sort of doubling-down on the initial anxiety-producing situation.

Medical intervention available today, such as antianxiety or antidepressant medications, can be beneficial with controlling anxiety. Counseling and group therapy, as an adjunct, can also help to facilitate recovery or alleviation of symptoms. These interventions may give you the ability to overcome or, at the very least, reduce your severe responses to stressors. Other relief-inducing strategies can include changing poor lifestyle habits, meditation and finding social outlets to help comfort anxiety responses.

Most who have experienced this emotion - whether mild or extreme - can agree that it is not pleasant or useful. It is distracting and downright devastating to the extreme. It is almost debilitating if we let it take hold and take over. As with anything, too much anxiety is killing us, but having a little of it might be beneficial if we don't allow it to take control of our minds and bodies. You need peace and calm when suffering from anxiety, but achieving it can be difficult when facing so many variables and constant stress. As we continue to understand what triggers us and how to diffuse those moments of anxiety, however, the process becomes easier.

Release Me, Oh Fiery Anguish

My body was calm, no more.
I'm surrounded and internally inundated with fear.
I'm swept up in it.

First one, then two, now a thousand thoughts hit my brain.
It has captured me.

The shocks begin to flicker throughout my body, my heart pumps frantically, my veins bulging with the surge.

I feel exposed and raw with this physical assault orchestrated by my mind.

All my focus is on how I feel just wrong.
I'm out of control in my own body.
I'm swimming in the verbal soup in my brain, and I'm drowning in it.
There's a disconnect in my reality.
Everything looks the same, but nothing feels the same.
I'm inside looking out, holding it together to find safety.

I hide, undercover, wishing it would go away, but just waiting for the next wave to hit.

I'm going to die.
I feel it, so it's true.

Sanity Lost

Life was for the taking; you bit off less than you could have. Fear kept you trapped.

Your journey was one of soothing, but numbing and banal repetition.

Reaching out for new experiences, challenging that fear was impossible.

Only mere moments captured some excitement, quelling and satisfying your deep yearning for more life.

It wasn't enough. You left this world unfulfilled.

I weep for you.

It Starts Yet Again

I'm thinking it over once more.
Really should try to stop that, I tell myself.

Not listening, again. I imagine what could be, not waiting for what will be.
I say it's in preparation...

"Hope for the best, expect the worst!"

Now I've gone and done it.
I'm in my head deep, fixated on the worst.
I feel awful. I let it go. It comes back.
Now I'm in for more.

A panic sets into my being.
I can't control the thoughts.
Whirling, whirling around, bouncing against all sides of my skull.

My chest feels tight; there's a weight on my head and buzzing in my being.
What feels like prickly electricity rages in every hair follicle on my body.
Every brush up against something sets off another charge.
Adrenaline is flowing.
I'm running in circles and going nowhere.

There is no escape.

I'm trapped and stuck in my mess of a head, the out of control chemicals surging in my brain. The once minuscule thought leads me to the edge of a deathly abyss. Every thought is pushing me to the fringe of sinking despair and irrational worry.

I'm dying now. But not really. Yes, really. No. YES!

Must. Go. To. The. Hospital... Now.
"You're having a panic attack."

I feel ashamed, guilty... worried. Meds on board, I'm better now.

But... I'm still afraid.

It'll start all over. Again.

Compassion

Those who are compassionate have a natural bent for it, and will instinctively volunteer where help is needed. People with this intention wish to remove the less fortunate from their condition of suffering, whatever that may entail. Many settings require people to naturally feel a strong sense of compassion for others, such as in hospitals, scenes of catastrophic disasters and animal shelters. The world we live in provides many opportunities to assist during times of devastating upheaval. Having compassionate people to attend to those in need is very beneficial and helps us to overcome grave situations; their caring and attentiveness in these times are helpful to the people who don't know what to do next.

As a species though, we aren't always compassionate. Maybe a person's previous actions make us dismiss our inclination to help them. Or, the person needing help may just be using us to avoid taking responsibility for a situation they created. We may waver on offering a helping hand because of judgment we've made about that person. We've all encountered individuals who are suspect of truly needing help. Hesitation usually follows this initial feeling of concern. In the end, if someone needs help, compassion often wins.

For a myriad of reasons, those who have been on the receiving end of this emotion may not always be grateful. Nonetheless, it is a kind thing to give of ourselves to bring some relief to the person who is suffering. Offering help sometimes comes at a substantial cost - both materially and emotionally - to the person providing that aid. Regardless, most of us will at least attempt to help create a positive outcome for someone in need.

I think many who are compassionate want and need a connection to those they are helping. It's not about 'feeling' needed. Rather, we are trying to extend our community by offering our sincere efforts to help. We want to surround ourselves with more people, and who better to include in that community than with those to whom we feel close? In feeling compassion, we are principally experiencing suffering along with the other person. At the same time, we get to share in the rejoicing when the pain is over. Sharing in these emotions makes the connection worthwhile.

Compassion in any form can be a powerful catalyst for good and, in some cases, compassion from others was the one thing to help get a person out of a truly horrific situation. That person's life was changed in essential and positive ways simply because someone cared enough to assist with that change. Compassion can help the disadvantaged have a new outlook on life, thereby empowering that person to continue making important decisions for their betterment. That person's successes can then impact other people in a similar situation. Or, it can help to identify areas where they need to make some improvement. Having compassion affects people in a positive fashion. In turn, it can create more opportunities to learn to overcome devastating events. It can also inspire others to help those in need. It can create the dynamic of *Pay-It-Forward.*

As long as there is life, there will be suffering. It is indiscriminate in what it doles out and how it unleashes its devastation du jour. Add to our world of natural disasters self-inflicted wounding, along with the mindless drama inflicted by others, and we've got a world full of hurt. What would it look like if the first emotion we felt when encountering others was that of compassion instead hesitation, doubt or apathy? We could all benefit from people being willing to help one another instead of tearing them down or ignoring them. A compassionate world is what we would call Utopia.

Communicating with Your Being

They can see it in your moist-filled eyes,
and your gentle touch.

It resonates to their core.

You gaze silently, speak quietly, comfortingly;
soothing the emotions of struggle with strengthening love.

Injury and distress require compassion;
it heals wounds left by tragedy.

Give it freely, and their world changes.

They will remember you,
and be eternally grateful for your care of them.

Helping them out of their darkness.

Your compassion spoke to their needs.
What initially connected you by misfortune,
forever binds you through humanity.

Forever.

You're deeply connected through suffering adorned with love
and resolve.

Their lives changed for the better.

All by the sympathetic gesture of your humanity, your depth of feeling compassion for others.

You are a game-changer.

You Needed Me

I can't turn away from the plight before me.
The instinct of good intentions rises from within.

You're at your wits end.
I'm determined.

Tell me what has happened, who did this or why it has occurred to you?

Let me provide comfort while you purge.
It'll be my first step toward righting this wrong.

There is a way out of this mess. I promise.
You may not see it. Yet. Or, even believe me now.

But I will help you.

You need me, and I'm there for you.

I will do what it takes to see you get back on your feet.

That's who I am.

For you, for everyone.

I Feel Better

I'm in a bad way.
You saw, you acted. I'm good.
Thanks for being there.

Interest

We are all naturally inclined to want to like someone. The charm of another person can take ahold of our senses, and we favor them. We become interested in them. Then we try to learn more to appease our curiosity. The same goes for a hobby or a cause. We give it attention because something within us is interested in whatever it is about it that spoke to our preferences and forged a connection. In some instances, it isn't just that our attention gets drawn in the direction of our interest. Rather, our focus on it can become quite pronounced. A commitment to it is the definition of championing a cause. Activism was born out of initial interest. What will keep the attentiveness going is the desire to see that cause get satisfaction, whatever that need may be.

Interest is not always just having a desire to know about an individual or a cause. Sometimes it can be a thing. Being quizzical about its function, what it contributes and what it does. It's about exploration, feeling an urge to know more than before and always questioning, wanting answers. It is the initial interest in something that builds the foundation for gaining more knowledge. It is to be wholly involved in whatever has piqued our curiosity. It is somewhat of an introduction to a conclusion of sorts; the result being the answer to our curiosity. Having the interest may never cease, even when you reach a point of clear understanding. This clarity just spurs us on to find new ways of applying what we know.

It's a good thing to show interest. Looking at our world, it's evident it exists. Just look at our history and where we started. Imagine our world if there was no interest or curiosity! Progress comes from being interested, and our society changes directly because of it. Contributions to our culture come from those people who are most in-tune with that which stirred their interest. People will often try to follow career paths that align with their interests. Their choices are partly seen by the lines of work, types of industry or subjects they pursue, but also by the areas where they tend to excel because those areas held their attention. Hobbies further fill the desire for being immersed in something that gives satisfaction and makes us better versions of ourselves.

Interest is what keeps us engaged in our world. It's what arouses, intrigues and fascinates us in our surroundings. It can create an excitement within us, making us feel more connected and alive. Without it, what is the reason for even being here? It would seem a dull existence would be our fate if we were unable to be attentive toward anything other than ourselves.

Lacking the Interest

Life is a constant entanglement requiring my effort.
I don't choose to accomplish goals.
I don't show interest to engage in anything other than what is required of me to sustain.

I let life happen to me and give it the appropriate response.
That's it.
I'm just here taking up space.

That's dangerous.
I'm not liked because I show no interest in anything.
But it works for me.

Life, situations, people, whatever....
They all happen to me, not because of me.

I'm afraid.
Too much thinking, too much involvement, too much drama...
It will only end badly.

I relinquish my contribution to resolutions, to engagement.

Intrigued

It has captured me,
Instilled an intense craving.
I want to know more.

Your Attention

It's the little things I notice.
They're only for me.

Every act of inserting your life into mine tells me you are aware of me.
You want to be.

A call here and there.
The short text now and then, emojis sprinkled throughout.
Small notes to show you care.
The occasional thoughtful gift, all rewards of being your focus.

Knowing I cross your mind feels satisfying, like being put up on a pedestal even when you are not close enough to lift me.
Diligent care delivered at just the right moment.

The hard moments for me only double your call of duty; your presence alone can ease them, but your acts of kindness help to erase them.

I feel so good being wrapped up in your love and attention, a warm blanket of comfort.
Tattered and torn by age, but possessing strength and resilience.

It surrounds me.

Acceptance

Acceptance doesn't always come easy. It can be a struggle to identify or embrace things we internally disagree with. Eventually, many of us strive to achieve some peace and rest from the turmoil that comes when we can't accept things about people, what is happening around us in our world or even when we don't accept ourselves for who we are. Whether it be any of those - understanding, welcoming reality, acknowledging and approving of the rights of others - acceptance helps to create an atmosphere of calm. It gives us a much better starting point for moving forward in a healthy and rational way. We'll make better decisions when we can accept our situations, ourselves and the people around us.

Accepting Each Other
When we can remove the emotional attachments we have to what makes us different, it helps us as individuals and influences groups to be more collaborative and productive. Our egos will naturally try to make us feel more superior of our opinions or lifestyle choices and, of course, less accepting of others. Lack of acceptance is the struggle, but it's worth getting through to the other side. Conflict ceases to be the main issue that controls our lives when we realize we are only challenging rather than embracing and understanding. Accepting is the first step in identifying that we want more than just our ego to call the shots. If the end game is for us all

to benefit, we finally understand that engaging in endless conflicts is not the most productive option.

There will always be disagreements among people because there will always be differences. We wouldn't be human if that weren't the case. That doesn't mean we can't be accepting of others while we examine how to bridge the gap between those differences. Embracing what we might not agree with is a conscious choice. It can require some heavy-duty effort on our part at times, but it can be done. Our emotional attachments can create a bubble around us, thereby insulating the feelings that give us most comfort and attachment to issues. It can color our perspective to the point that we shun others. In this case, you only sincerely love your issue and the benefits you get from defending it. You have forgotten to love the person who resides in the other camp on that matter. Withholding approval is not helpful to either of you. Rather, it is just a continuation of the "I'm better than you" mentality. This form of arrogance is not acceptance. Rather, this is division, and it classifies the other person as being either bad or wrong. When you choose to look at these differences as a bad part of the other person, you are making a conscious choice not to be accepting.

When Life Treats You Unfairly

Devastating situations can make us feel out of control emotionally. We can then quickly become overwhelmed if we don't take steps to understand the reality of a situation and accept what is or is not going on. Giving in to your fear of the unknown and failing to understand the situation realistically undermines the good decision-making and level-headedness required at that moment. Accepting reality helps determine the next steps we need to take. Once we realize that many things are out of our control, we can focus on what we *can* do to help in the situation. Acceptance of our actual circumstances, rather than what we want them to be, helps us focus on achieving the next level or solving the next problem. Experiencing out-of-control emotions about things, not in evidence, including anxiety, worry, and fear, does not help the situation. Understanding these feelings and why you are experiencing them is all part of accepting reality. This acceptance of reality grounds us. The ability to overcome horrible situations requires a clarity of what needs to happen next. Understanding is only achieved by first accepting what is going on.

Accepting Yourself

The individual journey we each make through life can sometimes be fraught with a dislike of who we are. Whether it is a rejection of our physical selves, problems created by our behaviors or feeling like we don't fit in with the right people, we feel like we just don't matter. We question our existence, and we deny a unique love and relationship with ourselves.

Do we all feel some things could be better about us? Absolutely! Until we can claim ourselves and love who we are, we will be unable to change the things about ourselves that bother us. Think about any situation where we didn't like something or someone. Was there excitement or an inclination to help? Probably not. We hinder honest individual growth and maturity when we haven't first acknowledged and accepted who we are. It is only then that change can happen. Self-worth and loving yourself gives you the courage and commitment you need to become who you think you should be. It isn't easy, for sure, but in the end, the person we proudly see reflected in the mirror is someone we fight for willingly.

Much of what shapes our thinking about ourselves and dismissal of our uniqueness is the idea that someone else decides what makes us notable. Others don't get to determine that. We have to decide what we like, what we love and what we admire about ourselves. We also have to decide what we don't like about ourselves so that we can accept both the good and the bad. These traits are what make each of us unique. You hold the power to be the individual you want to be, and you control the person who you are at this very moment. Owning who you are is real acceptance. Feeling shame or lacking self-worth will continue if you do not fully embrace the individual that you are. We can go a long way when we understand *"This is who I am, right here, right now and I'm as good as I can be at this moment."*

Feeling Accepted

When we find people who look at us with nothing but 'hurray for you!' eyes... well that's a place called *'feeling really at home.'* It's a calm space, a loving one that feels warm, almost fluid. We can be at ease with ourselves and our surroundings, whether in their arms or just in their quiet presence. When we find those people, we must hold on tight. They can teach us something, and we can learn volumes if we let them.

These exceptional people might be family, friends or even strangers. Their entrance into our lives can be the catalyst for good to show up at our doors. The ability to pay it forward through our actions only adds more greatness to this world. When we are accepted, we return the favor and continue the cycle of acceptance.

As we go through our life journey, we'll see who touched us and helped make it just a little bit better, even when we've veered off course due to devastating life situations. Deep down, if we are fortunate enough to have people in our life who supported, loved us unconditionally and mentored us, it meant we were accepted exactly for who we were. It gave us strength and understanding we might not even have realized until we were much older. Upon reflection, we see who was in our corner all along. We smile, and we feel thankful.

Showing the World, Me

The world sees what I show them. What's standing in front of them is their guide. But...

I'm crying on the inside. I'm dying.

My face tells another story, one the world around me will accept. They won't have to coddle, fix, help heal or just love; they wouldn't want to. It's better this way; it's what I tell myself.

Cracking the exterior. Letting the reality out, watching the ooze of ill project upwards and letting it fill the air. It's scary; it's shame-filled and guilt-ridden.

I imagine I'm exposed; people wouldn't understand. They wouldn't care. They wouldn't help. Belittling would occur. Anger would present itself; I'm scared. I stop and go further in, deeper where it's safe. Again, I lie to myself.

My despair deepens; the picture perfect is no longer untarnished. Moistened eyes remove the warm glow of feigned happiness. Deep dimples erased as frowns commandeer the territory of the face. The tears creating a river following their natural path. It doesn't seem to want to end. The floodgates have opened; I can't contain them any longer. I have to purge. I feel sick. I feel unable to control myself anymore. Still, it's necessary.

I was wrong; there are those who comfort me. They shield me while I let go of the hurt, the anger, the frustration. They hold me until it's all okay again. I'm back in the world that sustains me. My focus is clearer, my strength restored.

My real friends surround me; I can go back and take on the world.

Camouflage not necessary. Not anymore.

Will You Take Me as I Am?

Years of pretending, just to be accepted.
The agony behind the smiles, just to be accepted.
Negating who I was, just to be accepted.
It felt like what I should do, just to be accepted.
Where did it get me?
Friends and family who didn't like me, even when I gave them who they wanted me to be.

Today, I've gotten beyond the shell I created. I've fully emerged into who I need to be.
Today, my pretense falls away, and the joy of my real being previously held-in oozes out to greet this new life.
Today, I'm true to myself, true to who I am and who I want to be.

Will you be here tomorrow?

"To exist is to change, to change is to mature, to mature is to go on creating oneself endlessly." **- Henri Bergson**

I Don't Accept

It's wrong; you're wrong! You can't make me see it any other way when there is so much here to prove it to you. You're not listening! I want to make you understand; you won't let me! You're refusing to hear me! GRRRR!! This is so aggravating. You are only trying to shut me down. LISTEN TO ME!!!

"Would you rather be right or be loved?"

I grew up thinking it was an either-or thing, but it's not.

I can be both. I can accept being wrong, still loving the other. Telling someone that truth is worth dismissing to have love and acceptance mean truth doesn't matter, but it does.

The person who wishes to sweep the truth under the carpet is interested in only one thing: they are trying to convince you they are more important than you and that acceptance of you only hinges on what they want to know. You give them more than they can handle; the connection will be brittle. Eventually, it will break.

I don't accept the willful denial of what is the truth just to keep a sort of delusional idea of reality in place. Trying to maintain a relationship with someone who chooses their misconceptions over a connection with me is rather difficult. They don't accept me because truth scares them. That's okay.

I accept the idea that I won't be close with everyone. The world is full of people like me. I've found many who I can relate with and who accept me just because the truth is important.

Affection

Affection isn't just an emotional experience and response. Rather, it is an emotion expressed and felt physically.

Humans need touch. Some may require a lot of it; many don't need very much. Our bodies do much better when they are stimulated by touch, whether giving or receiving it. Many studies have demonstrated the body's positive responses to touch. It helps to lower blood pressure and heart rate, calms cardiovascular stress, activates the vagus nerve, increases immune function when relaxation response is triggered, relieves pain, makes us happier and less anxious and allowing us to unwind from the stresses of the day. Hugs can flood your body with oxytocin, which is considered the "bonding hormone." Touch can lower cortisol levels and reduce stress. Even self-touch indicates we will present with a lower risk of depression. Stroking the fur of pets releases tension, improves immune function and helps to lower blood pressure. It also helps ease pain or at least the perception of it. Babies have been shown to thrive with human touch. Without it, mortality increases dramatically. So much healing can occur with close physical contact. Affection is one of the most valuable emotions of humankind, and science confirms that physical affection continues to be a fundamental element of human communication, bonding, and health.

Being 'affected' by someone can make us feel consumed by and connected to them with their mere presence. It can border on lust in some cases. Affection is a physical response to someone we don't want to keep wrapped up inside ourselves. The urge to touch reaches out instinctively to that person who draws us out. It is a feeling of buoyancy in a heavy world when we know someone has affection for us and we have it for them. It's the secondary response to being in love. It's the physical response we have to let people know we like them, accept them and possibly love them.

We show affection in a variety of touch ways, such as kissing, holding hands, squeezing a shoulder in an assuring manner, hugging deeply or just through a quick, but firm handshake. We also demonstrate affection with loving gazes, giving gifts, and by meeting one another's physical and emotional needs. It's reciprocating love with love, accepting someone for who they are, feeling a genuine warmth for another being. The list is seemingly endless.

What humans try to communicate through touch and affection is how much compassion they have for another being. It communicates caring, love and trust through a generous application of this emotion, either verbally or nonverbally. It can say to the person *"I know how you feel."* It creates a bond for those involved, but also a sense of social well-being. It helps create a kinder, more compassionate and gentler society.

In the right situations, it is a wondrous thing to feel affection for someone or to be on the receiving end of it. Who hasn't come home at the end of a bad day and found a release in the arms of their loved one? Had their mood shifted ever so slightly when a toddler held their hand or looked into the smiling face of someone they admired only to feel that same uplifting feeling occur inside of themselves? Affection will demonstrate itself mostly through touch but experienced in so many different ways. Whichever way it is displayed or received, attention to us makes the atmosphere of our surroundings that much lighter and sweeter. It is the cushion of comfort separating us from that which would seek to muddy our current state of stillness and calm. It is a respite from the strife and anguish in our world. It is a form of love, and the gift to recharge our hope and desire to go on.

"To touch can be to give life." Michelangelo

I Touch, I Care

I'll always reach out when I see…

Sadness
Tears
Pain
Rage
Fear

I hope it gives you…

Joy
Comfort
Hope
Calmness
Peace

It does for me.

PDA

"Ewwww! Get a room, you guys!
P*erhaps a **D**ab of **A**ttention is what you are craving?*
Admit it.
Otherwise, why would you throw it in our faces?"

No, little ignoramus.

You must be deprived.

Only the jealous have a problem with **P**eople **D**elighting in **A**ffection.

I Feel Your Love

You awaken a softness in me. My world becomes less harsh. Sadness and the anxieties of the day slide off me when my thoughts reach for you.

I feel a rush of affection when I think of your beauty and your force. It radiates on the surface but originates deep within. You are a rare find - the layers of stunning within you explode outwards into view. It demands my attention.

Then I see you, and we both instinctively know we need each other to be connected, if only by clasping the other's hand. It's enough for now. Maybe.

When your eyes capture the goodness in me, your smile tells me I'm yours. My psyche shudders in return. A layer of softness surrounds my body when you look at me. I'm waiting for the moment when our physical caresses dominate the conversation. My arms around you, my lips on yours, our bodies connected by touch and the unseen.

Let the distance between us fall away. I want to feel your breath move along the path of your kiss upon my skin, the delicate hair moving ever so smoothly under the pressure of your gentle force. My hands long to sculpt your skin, endlessly. I need you.

Finally, your hand interlaced with my fingers. My other hand will touch your hair. I will brush my lips up against yours and lean into you for comfort.

I am at peace.

Anger

Who in this world hasn't felt justified in their anger after being wronged? We've all been on the receiving end of someone else's stupidity and ignorance. We have all felt anger when things have not gone as expected or after we have been hurt or betrayed by another, whether those behaviors were intentional or unintentional. We are truly human when we give in to our wounded feelings. We seek resolution for them and may demand rather than negotiate in those moments.

When angry, we can unexpectedly experience immediate aggression, prickliness, a sense of being on edge and, quite possibly, a complete removal of love and compassion for another. The body may feel hot, agitated or even bristly. It creates a sensation of electricity that flows through our body with no escape. Or, we may experience the exact opposite with no immediate or public reaction. A lack of emotional response to these situations is perceived as being 'cool, calm and collected' but internally, there may be a fire raging. The well-known phrase *"Silent, but deadly"* deals with the odiferous aftermath of quiet flatulence, but anger that is eerily suppressed could also have a rather unpleasant outcome.

Anger motivates us to speak out or to take action to right a wrong. Publicly expressing anger can help us to calm down, but only when we utilize it to bring about necessary change.

The resolution that follows will eliminate our emotional turmoil. When in private, some might explode to achieve an immediate release, just like a steaming kettle on a stove. Once it has boiled over and is off the heat, the situation is over. This emotion is a mechanism for bringing back rational thinking. At the same time, you have to be careful not to cling to the anger afterward. Continuing to ruminate in it, without taking the steps necessary to resolve the initial conflict, will not contribute to anything of value. You are only hurting yourself by remaining in a constant state of agitation. If you lack the courage to identify how you got to this place, you will never acquire the skills necessary to take the next logical steps toward achieving real change and gain satisfaction.

People's reactions to the stresses of a perceived injustice are all over the place. How they've become accustomed to managing with those moments of ire is dependent on past nurturing, their personality and taught coping skills. We will never know every intricate detail of their lives which influence their response to situations and their inclination to anger. What can be frightening are the expressions of full-on rage. We see the results of that play out in the local and national news, the Internet and even in our communities. Expressed unbridled fury has damaged so much in our societies and has contributed to hysteria in some situations from which it is grueling to recover.

In a perfect world, anger would have a place at the table, but hopefully a very limited course. Our relationships, our society, and our world need anger only to be the identifier of what has gone wrong in situations. It would only serve to advise you that an injury of some sort has occurred. Both the wronged and the wrongdoer must then work to understand the anger projected from the other side. In this way, it can be a productive emotion for bringing about a resolution, but only if all parties are mature enough to ensure it happens this way. When we realize where the anger comes from, our ego needs to take a backseat for the benefit of finding a solution as well as obtaining the ultimate goal: to find peace and harmony in our lives.

I Lose, I Triumph

I was worthy of a better, happier life than you deemed I was going to live.

Every time my name comes up, I hope you choke on it with irritation.

That's what you deserve: a lifelong aversion to the utterance of what once so effortlessly came across your lips.

I hope it makes your body fill with pins and needles whose friction tears you up on the inside.

You, the creator of your destruction.

I walk away comfortably knowing you'll bleed from the inside.

I am better without you.

Target of Your Rage

Thoughts not expressed remain imprinted on the canvas of your heart and the crevices of your brain.

Your body absorbing more and more.

Holding it in, holding it back. It's a recipe for an emotional hot mess.

Please share, it's easier to protect myself from a misting rather than a deluge.

Pretty Ugly Liars

You lied to my face.

It was so easy for you to do, justifications aplenty.

Oh, how many years I wasted on you.

That, I do regret.

You revealed yourself to me; finally, I understood.

It changed everything.

Something was wrong with me, you said.

But there wasn't.

I got your number; I ain't never dialing it again.

I don't talk to liars anymore.

Depression

One could describe depression, whether mild or severe, as being in a blank space with no energy, desire, motivation or strength. There is a sadness and loneliness with no hope that it will get any better. The life experiences, whether they are interactions with others or situations encountered during daily life, are tainted with a bleak outlook. Compounding the negative is a feeling of not knowing who to trust or who even to turn to if help is needed. One can feel emotionally drained and seemingly have no courage to go forward, feeling mired down and stuck in the current circumstance of their being. It is the feeling of waiting to be filled with aliveness.

For those who are fortunate to only suffer from mild depression, something most individuals contend with at least once in their lives, it can be a standard response to a devastating situation. It is the catalyst for change in their lives, a betterment of their current circumstance. The place they find themselves prompts a motivation to alter what is affecting them detrimentally. It is a healthy response in that situation. That is the positive of depression: insight gained during the down period that further propels you in the direction you want to go. You may even reach that goal sooner and more quickly than you previously thought. You are now in a better place because you now know how to avoid those situations in the future.

Depression can feel like being weighted down by the world. You may feel pressed into a deeper feeling of gravity, with steps feeling heavier and limbs not lifting as lightly as before. It's likely you may also feel the world is tinged with a bleak lens, coloring all incoming stimuli with a muted or darkened filter. Escaping from this dark place is difficult.

We all have an internal desire to be free of depression, whether the condition is brief or long-term. Like with any negative feeling, there is a drive to experience something less debilitating. Most, if not all, individuals would rather experience a sense of comfort and joy, rather than sadness and isolation. It feels rather difficult to overcome depression when enveloped by such strong feelings. Depending on the person, it can pass quickly. Sadly, there are those who experience it quite often and very profoundly with some facing depression as a constant condition. Depression becomes who they are rather than who they want to be.

It's been said that to move forward, you must go back a few steps. Each time, you gain more than what is lost. Depression acts like that, but will often leave you feeling as though more is lost than gained. This state is chiefly true for people with clinical depression. Once a situation seems to have been mastered, another comes along to slow the progress of existence. On it will go. Tragically, many of these cases can be lost to suicide if the pain never subsides.

Many would argue that our world is creating the massive depression that seems to be engulfing our civilization. With the rapid changes we experience technologically, our minds just can't seem to keep up with allowing our satisfaction levels to rise with it. Is it a lack of contentedness that contributes to the masses in our society being depressed? The progress creates ever-newer realities for us, challenging our ability to feel stable due to rapidly changing situations. It almost becomes elusive. Or, is the pollution in our world - the by-product of progress - a disruption to our natural physical state? Or, maybe depression is just a necessary part of life.

As with all emotions, depression can be helpful, and yet, devastating extremes exist. We can control it to some degree and sometimes we just cannot. It all depends on our chemical makeup and the influences or experiences in the lives we lead.

Wanting

I go through my day visibly displaying a lethargic struggle; it belies the want beneath.

The dense fog in my head, the burdensome weight of it keeps me trapped there. The motions (and emotions) I must go through are much heavier. To reach the end of my day, to have felt the slightest bit of satisfaction, contribution or be somewhat alive once again is arduous and only half as fulfilling as it could, or rather, should be.

I don't want to be there in that dark, lonely place of lows. The daily effort of maintaining the bare minimum for existence taps any and all reserves I have left. Who chooses this? No one.

I would choose ease. I would choose smiling. I would choose *having* a life. One that doesn't make me feel like I don't want go on.
But how do I get there? How can I escape something which continually pulls me down?

Beneath the despair, my trapped being aches to surge above the quagmire holding me in place. I felt good once; I know I did. When did it fade away into faint, distant feelings of once having fun in my life?

I want it back. I want to be wholly immersed and bathing on the flip-side of my current state. *I want joy back.*

But my depression wants something else for me.

Who am I going to let win?

You Did This to Me

When my trembling hand put down the phone, my eyes quickly filled. The tears began to fall.

Slowly, at first. Then torrentially pouring out of me. My face, my hands covering it, my heaving chest, my legs and even my toes doused with the liquid misery I shed after hearing the news.

I wasn't part of our world of two anymore. You decided that. I had to live with it.

The sudden sharp turn life took in that moment was devastating and incredibly sad. The deep ache of separation from you left me in shambles. For a long time.

Weeks went by where all I managed to do was present an empty shell of a person at work, just getting by with the minimum of contribution. Just barely enough to keep my job. Every minute outside of it spent in mourning and sadness. I cried myself to sleep every night, only to wake up and complete the cycle again.

I didn't eat. Nothing tasted as good as the sweet kisses I would recall so easily, crying all over again when I realized I couldn't have them anymore. You made sure of that.

I was so lonely. I missed you so much. Your hands reaching out and touching mine, your warm embrace, your body nestled up close. Never again would I feel you around me, next to me or with me. You broke me in half. ***You*** did this to me.

This incredible sadness enveloped me, tainting every experience as I continued to move forward without you. It colored my world bleak for what seemed like forever. The enthusiasm for it was just gone. I didn't run my life; my emotions were running me... into the ground.

But slowly, with time, somehow, I began to miss you less. A lightness returned to my world, creeping in one ray at a time. I started to re-engage with my friends and smile. I began to direct my focus and energy back to me and away from you. Just like you wanted.

But I didn't do that for you. I did it *for* me.

Longing for an End

Days past appear at the door of my present. They push inside to fill the heaviness in the room.
Slowly, reluctantly a smile begins to form across my weary face.

Uninhibited laughter, passionate entanglements, mundane and easy tasks; all flickering a pretty picture.

Actively watching the glorious memories, slightly faded, now vividly replaying in my mind.
Hope glimmers slightly, will they fill up the chasm of emptiness?

But the door closes eventually. I'm again fully toiling in the sorrow which summoned another life.
I'm once again where I don't wish to be.
Tears, uninvited, fall silently. The wetness glazes over the joy just experienced during my reflection. My mind so quickly shifts back to the bleakness I was trying to escape.

I'm still alone. I'm still sadly cowering under the blanket; pillow clutched tightly smelling of moist misery. I wish to have this black cloud surrounding me dissipate. Let me feel like I can take in a deep breath of calm and ease, just one.

I roll over and beg for sleep to come, to still the ache deep within. There is no strength or courage, no desires to fulfill. Just a need to not feel this way anymore.

But do I get there... no. I just keep sinking down deeper and deeper into the hole freshly created for me. There is no light; there is no hope.

I'm in the folds of darkness. The despair is just too much, too overpowering now.

Please! I need to be released from this place where my mind is the evil warden, and my body is my prison. Now.

I just can't do this anymore...

Conclusion

Now you understand why people have always fascinated me - the full richness as well as the devastating ugliness of them. This book was just one small way for me to delve a bit deeper into what their stories look like, what feelings they comprise and what they ultimately mean. I'm glad I investigated what it is about life that brings people to feel emotions. What can I learn from others, and how can this insight influence me to move in a better direction for myself? I've learned so much from people's stories over the years. I hope that I will continue to grow into my own story, surrounded by the expression of others and the lessons I can capture from them. In many ways, their emotions push mine to the surface where it leaves me with only two options: either ignore them or learn from them. I've learned the hard way that ignoring is usually not the best thing to do, as emotions always seem to come up at the wrong time, and in the most inappropriate way.

Maybe that's why it was so relevant to me to write this book now. I'm at a point in my life where proper understanding and peace seem to be the highest goals. Much of who I am today is the result of the experiences I've lived and the emotions that have propelled me through those moments in my life.

I can only enjoy this understanding and peace if I learn to appreciate, examine and explore the emotions within myself;

and settling them, if need be. As I embark on this journey, there will be hurdles that appear impossible to overcome. Knowing myself, understanding my own emotions and having insight will help to minimize my emotional response, so it is not detrimental to me. I'd like to think I'm safeguarding my psyche or practicing self-preservation by delving deeper into the human condition. Some may think it foolish or even risky because it involves ripping open old wounds, which will only produce more emotions. I'm willing to take that chance. I'll be in a much better place once I've gotten to the other side of what pulls me down. Not only does it feel victorious, it feels empowering in preparation for similar future events.

Reflecting back now, I contribute much of what drove me to write this book to my relationship with Terry Susi, the book's artist. Our friendship began when we were just children. Our lives collided because we were the 'smart ones' in our 7th grade English class. What was a forced introduction, quickly turned into an easy and meaningful friendship. Although we only had four years together before she moved away, the connection we etched was life-long. We've been separated by many states ever since and, for years, out of touch with each other. Each was living our lives amidst struggles, joy, bad and good times - every emotion you can imagine and more. Interestingly, we both came out to be women who are strong, independent and kind. We didn't share much of the history we created apart from one another. In finding each other again, much of what we learned and faced together in our dysfunctional childhoods helped to shape our future. I hadn't realized how crucial this one relationship was to my survival until we reconnected again. It made me realize how much all emotions and life experiences contribute to the decisions we make and who we become. Most assuredly, I am a better person to have been influenced by my dear friend Terry during my formative years. This relationship and the mentoring we absorbed from each other gave us both a head start toward how we would deal with our futures. The beginning of our lives was rocky for us, but we've come full circle, Terry, and I. The place we are in now makes it all worth the pain we initially experienced. We watched ourselves blossom into understanding life, finding our place in it and enjoying much of what was in our control.

I hope I was able to convey the message of what being and feeling human is like, if only just a small but relevant sampling of it. This deeper investigation into human emotions, what we all so richly experience throughout our lives - the ups and the downs - are so different yet similar for all of us. Yes, we all have different experiences and the depth to which we experience them can set us so far apart, but the fact that we all do, in some form, identify with the same emotions connects us. Feeling human means, we need to tread lightly at times. Let's be kind and gentle as we go through our journeys, which will inevitably overlap with the journeys of others. Those we meet on our life's road trip are also walking on their path. They are experiencing it in their way, but in a similar vein as yours. I hope this can set you on a journey of self-discovery, allowing you to find a deeper understanding of yourself. A certain clarity for yourself which you deserve. More importantly, may it give you the opportunity to show the world the best *you* that you can feel.

~ Peace ~

A NOTE ABOUT THE AUTHOR

Susi Bocks is constantly evolving into more roles as her life continues towards its inevitable end. Many admirable hats have been worn throughout her existence, and some have come to an end. She's been a daughter, a sister, a friend, a wife, a mother, an aunt, a sister-in-law, a daughter-in-law, a paid worker in the capitalistic system in our world, a business person, and a volunteer for many worthy causes over the years. The current role of writer and author is hopefully not the last step in the journey that began as a blank slate. She lives smack dab in the middle of the United States.

Reach out and connect at IWriteHer.com

Made in the USA
San Bernardino, CA
11 January 2018